SKJC
2014

SUPER SIMPLE
NATURE CRAFTS

super simple
Leaf Projects

FUN AND EASY CRAFTS INSPIRED BY NATURE

Kelly Doudna

Consulting Editor, Diane Craig, M.A./Reading Specialist

A Division of ABDO

ABDO
Publishing Company

visit us at www.abdopublishing.com

Printed in the United States of America, North Mankato, Minnesota
102013
012014

 PRINTED ON RECYCLED PAPER

Editor: Liz Salzmann
Content Developer: Nancy Tuminelly
Cover and Interior Design and Production: Kelly Doudna, Mighty Media, Inc.
Photo Credits: Kelly Doudna, Shutterstock

The following manufacturers/names appearing in this book are trademarks: Craft Smart®, Crayola®, Elmer's®, Kittrich®, Mod Podge®, Pyrex®, Sunmark®, Tulip®

Library of Congress Cataloging-in-Publication Data
Doudna, Kelly, 1963-
  Super simple leaf projects : fun and easy crafts inspired by nature / Kelly Doudna ; consulting editor, Diane Craig, M.A./reading specialist.
     pages cm. -- (Super simple nature crafts)
  Audience: Age 5-10.
  ISBN 978-1-62403-079-6
1. Nature craft--Juvenile literature. 2. Leaves--Juvenile literature. I. Title.
  TT873.D68 2014
  745.594--dc23
                              2013022898

Super SandCastle™ books are created by a team of professional educators, reading specialists, and content developers around five essential components—phonemic awareness, phonics, vocabulary, text comprehension, and fluency—to assist young readers as they develop reading skills and strategies and increase their general knowledge. All books are written, reviewed, and leveled for guided reading, early reading intervention, and Accelerated Reader® programs for use in shared, guided, and independent reading and writing activities to support a balanced approach to literacy instruction.

TO ADULT HELPERS

The craft projects in this series are fun and simple. There are just a few things to remember to keep kids safe. Some projects require the use of sharp or hot objects. Also, kids may be using messy materials such as glue or paint. Make sure they protect their clothes and work surfaces. Review the projects before starting, and be ready to assist when necessary.

KEY SYMBOLS

In this book, you will see some warning symbols. Here is what they mean.

HOT!
You will be working with something hot. Get help!

SHARP!
You will be working with a sharp object. Get help!

contents

Lovely Leaves

We love the swish of leaves rustling on the tree. We love the crunch of fall leaves under our feet. But we don't love raking them. That's when it's time to get creative! Collect the colored leaves of fall and put them to use. Try the fun and simple projects in this book. The skies outside may be gray, but these leafy crafts will add some color inside!

About Leaves

The parts of a tree that are above ground are the trunk and the crown. The crown is made up of branches and leaves.

Leaves collect sunlight. Trees use the sunlight to make food. This process is called **photosynthesis** (foh-toh-SIN-thih-sis).

The leaves of many trees change color in the fall. A tree knows that winter is coming when there is less daylight. It stops making new food. It uses the food stored in the leaves. This makes the leaves change color.

fun fact

All trees have leaves. Even pine trees and fir trees have leaves. We call them needles.

fun fact

A tree with leaves that stay green all year is an evergreen tree. A tree with leaves that change color and fall off is a **deciduous** (dih-SID-yoo-us) tree.

CHOOSing LEAVES

We used fall leaves for the projects in this book. But green leaves will work just as well. Just choose leaves that are flat. You can use leaves from trees. You can use leaves from other plants. Many flowers have interesting leaf shapes. Look around at the different trees in your neighborhood. You will be surprised by how many kinds there are!

Preserving and Pressing

Different methods will give you different results.

Preserving with Glycerin

Soaking leaves in glycerin will make them soft.

1 Put the leaves in a baking dish.
Mix 1 part glycerin and 2 parts water.
Pour the glycerin mixture over leaves.

2 Put the foil pan on top of the leaves.
Press down to push the leaves under the liquid.

3 Let the leaves soak for three days.

4 Remove the leaves from the glycerin mixture.
Blot them with a paper towel. Let them dry.

5 (Optional) Press the leaves with the Weight Method (see page 9).

WHAT YOU'LL NEED

leaves
9 × 13-inch baking dish
glycerin
water
measuring cup
7 × 10-inch foil pan
paper towels

Preserving with Waxed Paper

Ironing leaves between sheets of waxed paper will make them flat and shiny.

1 Set the iron on high. Turn off the steam.

2 Lay one towel on the ironing board. Lay a piece of waxed paper on the towel.

3 Put a single layer of leaves on the waxed paper.

4 Lay another piece of waxed paper on top of the leaves. Lay the second towel on top of the waxed paper.

5 Iron the leaves for twenty seconds.

6 Flip everything over. Iron the other side of the leaves for twenty seconds.

7 Let everything cool.

8 Remove the top towel. Carefully peel off the top piece of waxed paper. Carefully remove the leaves.

 PRO TIP
Iron curly leaves for a few seconds before laying them on the waxed paper.

WHAT YOU'LL NEED

iron
2 thin towels
ironing board
leaves
waxed paper

Pressing with Weight

This is the easiest way to save leaves. You can also press leaves that you've preserved with glycerin or waxed paper.

1 Lay leaves in a single layer on a piece of paper. Put another piece of paper on the leaves.

2 Repeat step 1 to make more layers if you have more leaves to press.

3 **Stack** books on top of the layers. Leave in place for at least 24 hours. A few days is better.

WHAT YOU'LL NEED

leaves
paper
heavy books

WHat you'll need

Here are many of the things you will need to do the projects in this book. You can find some of them around the house or yard. You can get others at a craft store or hardware store.

leaves

measuring cup

9 x 13-inch baking dish

7 x 10-inch foil pan

ruler

clear contact paper

paper towels

thin towels

iron

waxed paper

foam brush

ironing board

paper

heavy books

rolling pin

1-inch (2.5 cm) paintbrush

scissors

solid-colored T-shirt

saucepan

baking sheet

oven mitts

fabric paint	acrylic paint	cardboard	white card stock	colored paper and envelopes

crayons	wide ribbon	flower pot	colored duct tape	small branch with forks

glycerin	craft glue	stick and pillar candles	empty can	all-purpose glue stick

Mod Podge	tall vase	hole punch	metallic thread	stones

polymer clay	round cookie cutter	wire coat hanger	toilet paper tubes	tape

DECORATED CANDLE

A classy candle adds an accent of light to any room.

WHAT YOU'LL NEED

leaves

craft glue

pillar candle

saucepan

water

white stick candle

empty can, cleaned and dried

1-inch (2.5 cm) paintbrush

1. Preserve some leaves using the waxed paper method (see page 8).

2. Put craft glue on the back of a leaf. Press it onto the pillar candle. Glue on more leaves.

3. Have an adult put 2 inches (5 cm) of water in a saucepan. Bring the water to a boil.

4. Break the white stick candle into pieces. Put the pieces in the empty can. Have an adult put the can in the pan. Simmer until the wax melts.

5. Brush the melted wax over the leaves on the pillar candle. Add more coats of wax until the leaves are sealed to the candle.

6. Let the wax cool.

 get fancy

Make a leafy ring to set your candle in. Trace around the bottom of the candle on a paper plate. Cut out the circle. Glue preserved leaves to the paper ring. Set the decorated candle in the middle.

paint print t-SHirt

Paint a print for some leafy fashion.

WHAT YOU'LL NEED

solid-colored
T-shirt

cardboard

fabric paint

foam brush

leaves

1 Lay the T-shirt flat. Slip the cardboard into the shirt.

2 Brush a thick coat of paint on a leaf.

3 Press the painted side of the leaf onto the shirt. Rub gently to **transfer** the paint onto the shirt.

4 Repeat steps 2 and 3 until your shirt looks the way you want it to.

get fancy

Try painting more than one color on each leaf.

note cards

Your notes will be more noteworthy with these colorful cards.

WHAT YOU'LL NEED

WHAT YOU'LL NEED

white card stock, 8½ × 11 inches

colored paper, 8½ × 11 inches

scissors

leaves

crayons

all-purpose glue stick

colored envelopes, 5½ × 4¼ inches

1. Fold a piece of colored paper in half. Fold it in half again. Cut or tear along the folds. You will have four smaller pieces.

2. Place one small piece of colored paper over a leaf. Color over the leaf with a crayon. The leaf's outline will appear on the paper.

3. Fold a piece of card stock in half crosswise. Cut or tear along the fold. Set one piece aside.

4. Line up the right edges of the card stock and the leaf print. Glue the leaf print in place.

5. Fold the card stock in half. The leaf print is the front of the card. Pair the card with a matching envelope.

fun tip

Make more note cards. Tie some together with ribbon to give as a gift.

flower pot

Pamper a plant with this pretty pot.

WHAT YOU'LL NEED

leaves

foam brush

fabric paint

flower pot

Mod Podge

Sparkle Mod Podge

1. Press some leaves using the weight method (see page 9).

2. Paint the leaves with fabric paint. Let the paint dry.

3. Put Mod Podge on the pot. Put Mod Podge on the back of a leaf. Press the leaf onto the pot.

4. Add more leaves to the pot. Let the Mod Podge dry.

5. Brush a coat of Sparkle Mod Podge over everything. Let it dry.

 Pro tip

Fabric paint is softer than acrylic paint. It will make it easier to wrap the leaves around the pot.

place mats

Pretty place mats make dinnertime delightful.

1. Preserve some leaves using the waxed paper method (see page 8).

2. Cut two pieces of clear contact paper. Make them 18 by 12 inches (45.7 by 30.5 cm).

3. Peal the back off one piece of contact paper. Lay leaves on sticky side of the contact paper.

4. Peal the back off the other piece of contact paper. Lay it over the first piece. The sticky sides should be together.

5. Firmly press the layers together. Rub out the air bubbles.

6. Put duct tape around the edges. Fold the tape over the edges.

Pro tip

Cut the duct tape a little longer than the side. After you have folded the tape over, trim the ends. Repeat on the other three sides.

leaf tree

A decorated tree isn't just for the winter holidays.

WHAT YOU'LL NEED

leaves

small branch with forks

acrylic paint, white and colors

foam brush

white card stock

craft glue

Sparkle Mod Podge

scissors

hole punch

metallic thread

tall vase

stones

1. Preserve and press some leaves using the glycerin and weight methods (see pages 7 and 9).

2. Paint the branch white. Let the paint dry.

3. Paint the leaves. Use a few different colors. Let the paint dry.

4. Use craft glue to glue the leaves to the card stock. Leave space between the leaves. Let the glue dry.

5. Paint over the leaves with Sparkle Mod Podge. Let it dry.

6. Cut out the leaves. Leave a ⅛-inch (.3 cm) border of card stock around each leaf.

continued on the next page

7 Punch a hole at the top of each leaf.

8 Tie a piece of metallic thread through each hole.

9 **Tilt** the vase. Carefully put some stones in the bottom. Stand the branch in the stones.

10 Hang the leaves from the branches.

 Pro tip
Tie two or three sticks together if you can't find a small branch.

 get fancy
Loosely wind metallic thread around the branches to give them some extra sparkle.

leaf imprint coasters

Put a cool coaster between your drink and the table.

WHAT YOU'LL NEED

polymer clay, 2 ounces (57 g) per coaster

waxed paper

rolling pin

leaves

4-inch (10.1 cm) round cookie cutter

baking sheet

oven mitts

acrylic paint

foam brush

safety tip

After you use the baking sheet for clay, do not use it for food again.

1 Knead 2 ounces (57 g) of clay until it is soft.

2 Put the clay between two pieces of waxed paper. Use the rolling pin to flatten the clay. It should be ¼ inch (.6 cm) thick. Make it a little larger than the cookie cutter.

3 Lift up the top piece of waxed paper. Lay a leaf on the clay. Replace the waxed paper. Roll over the wax paper to press the leaf into the clay.

4 Remove the top piece of waxed paper. Remove the leaf.

 Pro tip

Use a plastic lid in step 5 if you don't have a cookie cutter. Lay the lid over the leaf imprint. Trim the clay around the lid with a knife.

5 Center the cookie cutter over the leaf imprint. Press down to cut out a circle.

6 Lift up the cookie cutter. Remove the scraps of clay from around the circle.

7 Cover the baking sheet with waxed paper. Carefully lay the clay circle on the baking sheet.

8 Repeat steps 1 through 6 for each coaster. Place them all on the baking sheet.

9 Bake the clay according to the instructions on the package. Let the coasters cool completely.

10 Paint around the outside of the coaster. Don't paint inside the leaf print.

fall wreath

Fabulous fall colors make a splash on any door or wall.

WHAT YOU'LL NEED

leaves

wire coat hanger

12 toilet paper tubes

acrylic paint

foam brush

scissors

tape

craft glue

wide ribbon

1 Preserve the leaves using the glycerin method (see page 7).

2 Bend the coat hanger into a circle. The hook will be top of the wreath.

3 Paint the toilet paper tubes. Let the paint dry.

4 Cut a 2-inch (5 cm) **slit** in the middle of each tube.

5 Push the tubes onto the hanger. Fill the circle all the way around.

continued on the next page

6 Put tape over the **slit** in each tube.

7 Turn the hanger and tubes over. All of the taped sides should face down.

8 Glue leaves to the toilet paper tubes. Cover the entire circle.

9 Tie the ribbon into a bow. Glue it to the top of the wreath.

 Pro tip

Grouping leaves together makes it easier to fill in the circle. Glue a few small leaves to a large leaf. Then glue the group of leaves to a toilet paper tube.

conclusion

Aren't leaves great? You have let the beauty of nature come through with these wonderful leaf crafts. If you had fun, don't stop here. How else can you use leaves?

And check out the other books in the Super Simple Nature Crafts series. You'll find projects that use ice, pinecones, pressed flowers, seashells, and twigs. The ideas are endless!

glossary

deciduous – having leaves that fall off in the autumn and grow back in the spring.

photosynthesis – the chemical process that lets plants use light to turn water and carbon dioxide into food.

slit – a narrow cut or opening.

soak – to remain covered in a liquid for a while.

stack – to put things in a pile.

tilt – to make something lean or tip to the side.

transfer – to pass from one thing or place to another.